# Leaders & Managers

**SpiritBuilt Leadership 5**

Malcolm Webber

Published by:

**Strategic Press**
www.StrategicPress.org

Strategic Press is a division of Strategic Global Assistance, Inc.
www.sgai.org

2601 Benham Avenue
Elkhart, IN 46517
U.S.A.

+1-574-295-4357
Toll-free: 888-258-7447


Copyright © 2002 Malcolm Webber

ISBN 978-1-888810-44-8

All Scripture references are from the New International Version of the Bible, unless otherwise noted.

Printed in the United States of America

# Table of Contents

Introduction ........................................................................................... 7

1. Two Orientations ............................................................................. 9
2. The Differences ............................................................................. 11
3. Some Exercises & Applications ................................................... 23
4. The Roles and Responsibilities of Spiritual Managers ............ 37
5. The Skills of Spiritual Managers ................................................ 47
6. The Biblical Basis of the Distinction Between
   Leaders and Managers ................................................................. 57
7. Practical Implications of the Distinction Between
   Leaders and Managers ................................................................. 61

# Introduction

This is the fifth in a series of books on leadership. Together, they comprise the series, *SpiritBuilt Leadership*.

In this book, there are some opportunities for guided reflection. When you do these exercises, please go beneath the surface of your automatic reactions and be as honest with yourself as possible.

It will be most beneficial to study this book with others in a small group. That way you can learn and reflect together.

Our prayer is that this series of books will be effective in assisting Christian men and women around the world to be the mighty leaders God has called them to be.

*Malcolm Webber, Ph.D.*
*Strategic Press*
*Elkhart, Indiana*

# chapter 1

# Two Orientations

Leaders manage and managers lead, but the two activities are not synonymous.[1] Leadership and management are different.[2] They are distinctive and complementary. Each has its own functions and characteristics. Both are necessary for the organization to fulfill its divine purpose.

Many pastors are great spiritual managers. They are excellent shepherds. They love people and have well-developed "people skills" that enable them to minister one-on-one in sensitive situations. They genuinely care about the people and find satisfaction in helping them work through their problems. They effectively lead the Sunday morning meeting, putting together a program that will inspire, challenge and invigorate the people. During the week they are available to counsel, comfort, and help the people work through their problems. Certainly, this is not bad, but it is not necessarily "leadership."

Management is a set of processes that can keep a complicated organization of people running smoothly. Leadership is a set of processes that creates organizations in the first place or changes them to be what they could or should be.

Management deals with complexity. Leadership deals with change.

Leaders are visionaries. They think about the "big picture" issues of the long-term future. Managers are more concerned with making things work now.

---

[1] Many times, seminars and books on "leadership" are actually concerned with issues of management and administration.
[2] We are treating leadership and management here as "orientations" rather than as giftings or callings. Therefore, someone could be a pastor, teacher, evangelist, prophet, or apostle with the specific orientation of leader or manager.

The following diagram compares leadership with management, showing time against detail of activity.

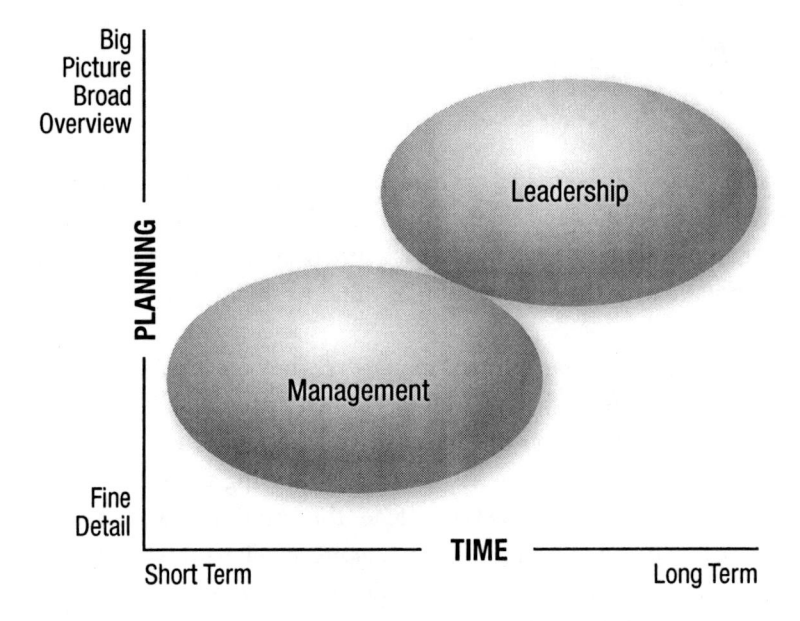

```
PLANNING
Big Picture / Broad Overview
    ┌─────────────────────────┐
    │           Leadership    │
    │    Management           │
    │                         │
Fine Detail
    └─────────────────────────┘
       Short Term    TIME    Long Term
```

It is obviously important that both ovals receive attention. If everyone spends all his time on visionary thinking (top right-hand corner), there will be plenty of dreaming but no action. However, if the sole area of concern is the bottom left-hand corner of the diagram, there will be much activity without integration, cohesion, direction or long-term purpose.

Someone said, "Action, without vision, is just passing the time. Vision, without action, is dreaming." A healthy organization needs both leaders and managers!

## chapter 2

# The Differences

Both leaders and managers deal with the same basic issues of direction, alignment and achievement,[3] but they approach them differently. Leaders and managers will also have significant personal differences.

The next four sections deal with these differences between leaders and managers. Incorporated into these sections is an exercise that will help you see where you are on the continuum between leader and manager. There are lists of the characteristics of leaders on the left side of each table and the characteristics of managers on the right side. In between, there is a space in which you can assess yourself on these characteristics. As you meditate on the specific differences between leading and managing, please think about how you usually function and write "leader" or "manager" in the middle space according to what best represents your thoughts and behavior. If you favor neither one, leave it blank. If you are very clearly one or the other, then please write either "leader" or "manager" and circle it.

There are no right answers. Please be honest with yourself. The answers you give will form an inventory for your own self-analysis.

## Direction

Both leaders and managers are concerned with providing direction for the organization but there are differences.

Management gives direction in the short term regarding the details. Leadership gives direction in the long term regarding the big picture.

---

[3] These three aspects of leadership were explained in *Leadership: SpiritBuilt Leadership #1*.

Management focuses on implementation: establishing detailed plans and schedules for achieving specific results, then allocating resources to accomplish the plan. Leadership calls for creativity: developing a compelling vision of the future and far-sighted strategies for producing the changes needed to achieve that vision.

Good management keeps an eye on the bottom line and short-term results, whereas leadership means keeping an eye on the horizon and the long-term future.

Management produces a degree of stability, predictability, order and efficiency. Thus, good management helps the organization achieve short-term results and meet the expectations of various people both inside and outside the organization. Leadership means questioning and challenging the status quo so that flawed, outmoded or irrelevant norms can be replaced to meet new challenges. Thus, good leadership can lead to extremely valuable changes that help the organization fulfill its divine purpose.

Management is needed to help the organization meet its current commitments, whereas leadership is needed to move the organization into the future.

Leaders build bridges to the future. Managers help us to actually get there.

Now, please assess yourself regarding these characteristics.

| Direction |||
|---|---|---|
| **Leaders** | **Your Assessment** | **Managers** |
| Focus on the long-term; watch the horizon | | Focus on the short-term; watch the bottom line |
| Create vision and strategy | | Plan and budget |
| Provide vision by working from the future back to the present | | Provide plans and goals by working from the present forward to the future |
| Ask "What?" and "Why?" | | Ask "How?" and "When?" |
| Identify opportunities | | Identify obstacles |
| Seek opportunity and improvement | | Seek predictability and continuity |
| Help people move from where they are now to somewhere else | | Help people succeed where they are |
| Define the path | | Clear the path |
| Ignite fires | | Initiate programs |
| Take risks | | Avoid risks |
| Start revolutions | | Protect the status quo |
| Create (often radical) change | | Maintain stability |
| Excited by change | | Threatened by change |
| Seek revolutionary change tied to future opportunity | | Seek incremental change tied to present demands |

| Direction | | |
|---|---|---|
| **Leaders** | **Your Assessment** | **Managers** |
| Should qualify idealism with realism | | Should qualify pragmatism with idealism |
| Information base of feelings, emotions and ideas | | Information base of data and facts |
| "If it's possible, let's do it!" | | "If it's necessary, let's do it." |
| Start new things | | Finish what the organization is already doing |
| Prioritize future challenges and opportunities | | Prioritize current commitments |

**Evaluation =**
(Generally speaking, do you think and function as a leader or manager?)

# Alignment

The issue of alignment involves helping the people to understand and embrace the direction.

Management is concerned with organizing a structure to accomplish the plan; helping the right people to find their right places within that plan; and developing policies, procedures and systems to direct the people to fulfill the plan. Managers are the thinkers who help others to do.

Leadership is concerned instead with communicating the vision and developing a shared culture and core set of genuinely-shared values that can lead the organization to the desired future. This involves others as thinkers and doers, with the leaders themselves fostering a sense of ownership within everyone. The vision describes the future, while the culture and values help define the journey toward it. Leadership focuses on getting everyone lined up in the same direction.

Managers organize by separating people into specialties and functions, with clear boundaries separating them by department and hierarchical level. Leaders break down boundaries so people know what others are doing, can coordinate easily, and feel a sense of teamwork, equality and overall purpose in fulfilling God's will.

A good clue in looking for leadership potential is to look for the ability to think across departmental issues, not just the ability to make out a strong case for one department. When it comes to the allocation of resources, leaders have to prioritize between multiple, well-presented, legitimate causes. One can only do this against a "big-picture" vision that covers the entire scope of the organization. Good managers make good cases for their own departments, but often cannot see, or hear, the validity of parallel claims on resources.

| Alignment | | |
|---|---|---|
| **Leaders** | **Your Assessment** | **Managers** |
| Start with the person and then determine the broad role he should play | | Start with the specific task and try to find the right person who will make a good "fit" |
| Think about people in terms of their growth and potential | | Think about people in terms of their fit with structures and procedures |
| Promote opportunities for growth | | Set and communicate the standards of successful performance |

| Alignment |||
| --- | --- | --- |
| **Leaders** | **Your Assessment** | **Managers** |
| Create vision and meaning for the organization and strive to transform culture | | Act within established culture of the organization |
| Embrace the big picture | | Focus on the details |
| Build broad ownership of the vision | | Get the right people in the right places |
| Pursue follower commitment | | Seek follower compliance |
| Idea-centered | | Plan-centered |
| Innovate for the entire organization | | Administer subsystems within the organization |
| Create shared values and culture | | Organize and delegate |
| Pursue creative acquisition of resources | | Action limited by available resources |
| Eliminate boundaries | | Create boundaries |
| Think across departments | | Strengthen within departments |

**Evaluation =**
(Generally speaking, do you think and function as a leader or manager?)

# Achievement

The issue of achievement of the vision involves helping the people to start moving to fulfill the vision and then to continue moving in the right direction, so that God's purposes are fulfilled.

Management focuses on things like procedures and reports, and on taking the daily steps necessary to achieve the organization's goals. Leadership, on the other hand, focuses on encouraging and inspiring people to continue moving toward the vision.[4]

Management is involved in directing and overseeing the people so that they do the right things the right way, whereas leadership is concerned with helping others grow so that they can fully contribute to achieving the vision.

The management communication process usually involves providing answers, solving problems and directing others, whereas leadership entails asking questions, listening and involving others. Communicating direction and cultural values in actions as well as words is necessary for leadership to influence the people toward understanding the vision and supporting it.

A manager's relationship with others is likely to be more formal, relying more on positional authority, than that of a leader. A manager will often see himself as an overseer or supervisor, whereas the leader sees himself as a mentor, coach or facilitator.

---

[4] Years ago, I attended a conference on cell churches that was organized by a large Asian church. The church's senior pastor led the main sessions and shared broad vision and purpose, greatly exciting the conference participants. However, when I attended a smaller session that was led by one of his team, the brother entered the room carrying huge manuals filled with sample reports, organizational charts and endless lists of procedures. With delight, he began to share all the fine details of an elaborate system and structure. The difference between leadership and management orientations was very obvious!

| Achievement ||| 
| --- | --- | --- |
| **Leaders** | **Your Assessment** | **Managers** |
| Concerned with maintaining alignment with the big picture | | Concerned with the details of the daily agenda |
| Inspire and encourage | | Direct and problem-solve |
| Seek ownership of the vision | | Seek performance |
| Release potential | | Coordinate people and resources |
| Encourage innovative thinking | | Encourage routine thinking |
| Find problems | | Solve problems |
| Question | | Tell |
| Focus on doing the right things | | Focus on doing things right |
| Seek effectiveness | | Seek efficiency |
| Model the way | | Explain the way |
| Coach | | Coordinate |
| Inspire | | Reward |
| Persuade | | Exchange |
| Use servanthood power | | Inclined to use reward, coercive and positional power |
| Transformational influence | | Transactional influence |

**Evaluation =**
(Generally speaking, do you think and function as a leader or manager?)

# Personal Qualities

Leadership is more than a set of skills; it relies on a number of subtle personal qualities that may be hard to see, but are very powerful.

Typically, managers have a low tolerance for ambiguity and are most comfortable in more stable, well-defined situations. Leaders, however, will be comfortable in the midst of rapid change, innovation, unclear authority, and broad-reaching empowerment.[5] This is a crucial distinction. Since a leader is so involved in the *future*, he must function effectively in an environment of some uncertainty – personal as well as organizational. The manager's focus, however, is primarily on the *present* so he functions well in a more certain environment.

Effective managers will be good at dealing with well-defined problems; for example, how to increase efficiency in a certain department. But leaders must be adept at handling problems that are nebulous or ambiguous, such as what is the future direction of that department in the midst of a changing external environment. The higher people rise in an organization, the fewer facts they typically have to inform their decisions.

Consequently, an ability to handle – and even thrive in – ill-defined and complicated situations is a critical leadership capacity. Many good managers become confused and hesitant in ambiguous circumstances, and try to delay their decisions until they have all of the available facts. Others are prematurely decisive when they ought to be more reflective. Effective leaders do neither. They are comfortable acting in gray areas and are often able to move forward in ill-defined and complex situations to the organization's advantage, seeing opportunity where others are only seeing confusion. This is a crucial distinction between leaders and managers.

---

[5] Years ago, I attempted to begin a ministry that involved a coalition of several pastors. The attempt failed because I was not able to describe the future of the proposed ministry with sufficient clarity to the participating pastors. What *was* sufficiently clear to me was not to several of them and the ministry never got off the ground.

Management can be more formal and distant in its relationships with others, while leadership means being emotionally connected to others. Where there is leadership, people are not merely performing tasks or activities; they become part of the community and feel that they are significant. Leaders deny their own desires for recognition, recognize the contributions of others, and let others know they are valued.

Sometimes, effective managers rely too heavily on systems, policies and procedures, rigidly expecting others to operate in the same manner. Such people can succeed in an organization until they rise to very senior positions, where their need for regimentation tends to alienate others and stifle creativity.

Management means providing answers and solving problems, whereas leadership requires the courage to admit mistakes and doubts, to take risks, to listen, to trust, to be vulnerable, and to learn from others. Emotional connections are risky but necessary for true leadership to happen.

Good leaders will have an open mind that welcomes new ideas. Moreover, they are willing to be nonconformists, to disagree and say no when it serves the larger good, and to accept nonconformity from others rather than try to squeeze everyone into the same mind-set. They will step outside the traditional boundaries and comfort zones, take risks, and make mistakes in order to learn and grow.

Good leaders will be honest with themselves and others to the point of inspiring trust. They will set high standards by doing the right things, rather than just going along with standards set by others.

Because leaders are so vulnerable, take risks, and initiate change (which typically encounters resistance), leadership causes wear and tear on the person. Therefore, leaders must be tough.

| Personal Qualities |||
|---|---|---|
| **Leaders** | **Your Assessment** | **Managers** |
| Comfortable with ambiguity | | Like certainty |
| Listen | | Talk |
| Open mind | | Expert mind |
| Emotional connectedness | | More formal relationships |
| Oriented toward people and concepts | | Oriented toward programs and procedures |
| Nonconformity | | Conformity |
| Seek flexibility | | Seek clarity of structure and procedures |
| Skilled in diagnosis, conceptualization and persuasion | | Skilled in technical competence, supervision, administration |
| Abstract and conceptual | | Concrete and well-defined |
| Decision making is intuitive and ambiguous | | Decision making is analytical and rational |
| Dislike inertia and boredom | | Dislike anarchy and surprise |
| Leadership is an art | | Management is a science |

**Evaluation =**
(Generally speaking, do you think and function as a leader or manager?)

## chapter 3

# Some Exercises and Applications

The distinctions between leaders and managers we have dealt with are conceptual. They may be difficult to apply to your life without specific examples.

## Exercise 1

To help you visualize more clearly the differences between leaders and managers it is useful to think of people you know in these roles. Think about people in your own organization, corporation, school, church or some other group you're a part of.

1.  Please make two lists. First, list the leaders in your organization or group. Then, list the managers.

   **EXAMPLES OF LEADERS:**
   
   Name                    Position
   
   a. _____
   
   b. _____
   
   c. _____

d. _____

e. _____

f. _____


**EXAMPLES OF MANAGERS:**

    Name                  Position

a. _____

b. _____

c. _____

d. _____

e. _____

f. _____

2. Now place your own name on the appropriate list as a leader or a manager.

3. Please answer the following questions about your list and the people on it:

   a. Who was easier to identify in your organization – leaders or managers? Why?

   _____

   _____

   _____

   _____

   _____

   b. Did you list some people in both categories? What can you learn from this?

   _____

   _____

   _____

   _____

   _____

c. Did you list more people in one category than in the other? If so, which category and why?

_____

_____

_____

_____

_____

d. Does your organization tend to support leaders or managers to a greater extent? Why? What is the evidence of this?

_____

_____

_____

_____

_____

e. Where did you place your own name on this list? Why?

_____

_____

_____

_____

_____

4. Discuss your answers with the others in your small group.

   a. For those in your group who are also in your organization, share the names each person included in the list of leaders and managers. How do the lists differ? Discuss the perceptions within the group.

   _____

   _____

   _____

   _____

   _____

b. Explain where you placed yourself and why. Ask the group for feedback. Did they place you in the same category? The group should give each person feedback regarding his own self-perception.

_____

_____

_____

_____

_____

c. As a group, develop a list of the defining characteristics of both leaders and managers within your particular organization.

_____

_____

_____

_____

_____

# Exercise 2

Put your observations from the four tables in the previous chapter into the following grid:

| Issues | My Evaluation |
|---|---|
| Direction | |
| Alignment | |
| Achievement | |
| Personal Qualities | |
| **Overall Evaluation** | |

Discuss your overall evaluation with others in your small group, and also with people you know – your spouse, coworkers, superiors, subordinates, etc. Give them the opportunity to affirm or deny the validity of your own self-evaluation. Answer the following questions:

1. Did your overall evaluation surprise you? If so, why?

   _____

   _____

   _____

   _____

   _____

2. Was your overall evaluation confirmed by those who know you? What can you learn from this?

_____

_____

_____

_____

_____

3. Was your overall evaluation consistent with what you believe is God's calling on your life? If not, why not?

_____

_____

_____

_____

_____

4. When you evaluated yourself, you did so for your behavior in one particular organization of which you are a part. If you evaluated yourself for your behavior in another organization, do you think your overall evaluation would have been different? What can you learn from this?

_____

_____

_____

_____

_____

_____

# Exercise 3

Of perhaps greater significance than your overall evaluation are the items for which you were very clearly one or the other – the times when you wrote either "leader" or "manager" and circled it. These items reveal your areas of particular strength and weakness. Each item reveals both a strength and weakness. As we will discuss later, everyone will benefit by having both leadership and managerial skills to some degree. You should function primarily according to your strengths, but you must also work on your weaknesses. The more a leader works on his managerial skills the more effective he will become, and vice-versa. Therefore, this exercise reveals what your agenda for self-improvement should be.

Let's define this agenda now. Using your inventory as a foundation, in the space provided make lists of:

> Part A. Your areas of present strength, how you use those strengths, and more ways that you could use those strengths in the future.

> Part B. Your areas of present weakness, how those weaknesses hinder you, and how you could strengthen those weaknesses in the future.

> Part C. Behaviors you need to change, the present barriers to improvement and the existing supports that will help you in these areas.

These lists will show you where you need to focus your attention in the days to come.

## Part A – Personal Agenda for the Future Use and Development of My Leadership and Managerial Behaviors

| My Areas of Present Strength | How I Use These Areas Now | More Ways that I Could Use These Areas In the Future |
|---|---|---|
| 1. | | |
| 2. | | |
| 3. | | |
| 4. | | |
| 5. | | |
| 6. | | |

# Part B – Personal Agenda for the Future Use and Development of My Leadership and Managerial Behaviors

| My Areas of Present Weakness | How These Weaknesses Hinder Me Now | How I Could Strengthen These Weaknesses In The Future |
|---|---|---|
| 1. | | |
| 2. | | |
| 3. | | |
| 4. | | |
| 5. | | |
| 6. | | |

# Part C – Personal Agenda for the Future Use and Development of My Leadership and Managerial Behaviors

| Behaviors I Need To Change | Existing Barriers to Improvement in These Areas | Existing Supports That Will Help Me Improve |
|---|---|---|
| 1. | | |
| 2. | | |
| 3. | | |
| 4. | | |
| 5. | | |
| 6. | | |

Share your agendas with your colleagues, spouse, friends and the members of your small group. Ask them for feedback. Ask them if they can help you strengthen your behavior. If they have completed their own inventories, compare their results with yours. Give them feedback as well.

Are there common features in the agendas of your colleagues? If so, this may reveal biases and expectations in your organization. Note similarities and differences in the analysis of barriers and supports. Similar perceptions of barriers and supports among colleagues may indicate a pattern in your organization's culture that limits the growth of strong leadership or managerial behaviors.

**chapter 4**

# The Roles and Responsibilities of Spiritual Managers

While leaders are generally responsible for the big picture, managers are particularly responsible for a little piece of the puzzle – to see that it moves forward effectively and efficiently.

Spiritual managers[6] have roles that relate to people, information and decision making.[7] Each role represents activities that spiritual managers undertake to accomplish their responsibilities, as they help the organization as a whole fulfill its purpose. Each managerial activity can be explained in terms of at least one role, although many activities involve more than one role. The relative importance of each role may also vary from one kind of manager to the next.

Although it is necessary to separate the various components of the manager's responsibilities to understand his different roles and activities, it is important to remember that the real task of management cannot be practiced as a set of independent parts; all the roles interact in the real world of spiritual management – often chaotically so! Thus, the spiritual manager who only communicates never accomplishes much, while the manager who only "does" things ends up doing them all alone.

---

[6] We will use the term "spiritual manager" here since most of our readers are involved in distinctly Christian ministry.
[7] This model of managerial roles is loosely adapted from Henry Mintzberg (1973), *The Nature of Managerial Work*.

# People Roles

These relate to relationships with others, and require "people skills" on the part of the spiritual manager, as well as communication abilities and a heart that genuinely cares for people.

1. As **leaders,** spiritual managers are responsible for looking at the big picture of the organization and making their "piece of the puzzle" function as an integrated whole in the pursuit of its basic purpose. Consequently, they must envision and strategize regarding the future, give guidance to those they are responsible for, ensure they are motivated, and create favorable conditions to help them fulfill their purposes. This role pervades all spiritual management activities, and includes mobilizing, training, directing, praising, correcting, promoting and dismissing.

   Please think about your role and respond specifically. Your role as a *leader* includes:

   _____

   _____

   _____

   _____

2. Acting as **shepherds,** spiritual managers must give pastoral care to those under their responsibility.

   - Praying for them.
   - Concern for specific personal and family needs.
   - Seeing they fulfill their calling in God.
   - Seeing they have strong friendships and ministry relationships.
   - Support in times of crisis.
   - General care-taking. Visitation, encouragement, basic counseling, etc.

Please think about your role and respond specifically. Your role as a *shepherd* includes:

_____

_____

_____

3. Spiritual managers, as **liaisons,** must establish and maintain a web of relationships with individuals and groups outside of their area of responsibility, so that the whole organization stays integrated and cohesive. These information links will exist both inside and outside the organization.

   Your role as a *liaison* includes:

   _____

   _____

   _____

4. Spiritual managers represent their units as **figureheads,** and fulfill necessary social and legal duties on behalf of everyone they're responsible for. For example, they will sign documents (e.g., expense authorizations, contracts), preside at certain meetings and ceremonial events, and represent their unit before outsiders. The manager must participate in these activities even though they are usually of marginal relevance to their core purposes as managers.

Your role as a *figurehead* includes:

_____

_____

_____

_____

## Information Roles

These roles describe the activities used to develop and maintain an information network. Spiritual managers spend a lot of time talking to people in various contexts.

1. Spiritual managers need to know what is going on – both inside their organizational subunit as well as in the organization as a whole and outside the organization. As **monitors,** they continually seek information from a variety of sources – both systematically and opportunistically. They analyze this information to discover problems and opportunities, and to develop an understanding of outside events and internal processes.

    Your role as a *monitor* includes:

    _____

    _____

    _____

    _____

2. Spiritual managers have special access to sources of information not available to subordinates. Some of this information is factual and some of it regards the preferences of the organizational leaders. They must act as **disseminators** of this information. Some of it must be passed on to subordinates, either in its original form or after interpretation and editing by the manager.

   Your role as a *disseminator* includes:

   _____

   _____

   _____

   _____

3. As **spokespersons,** spiritual managers are also obliged to transmit information and express value statements to people outside their subunit. They must report to whomever they are accountable to. They will also sometimes represent their subunit before outsiders.

   Your role as a *spokesperson* includes:

   _____

   _____

   _____

   _____

# Decision Making Roles

These roles pertain to the events about which the spiritual manager must make a choice and take action. These roles often require conceptual as well as people skills.

1. Spiritual managers are constantly thinking about the future and how to get there. At the grass-roots level of the organization, they are the **agents of change.** As they become aware of problems they must search for ways to correct them. Moreover, they must seek to continually improve their unit so it can best serve the organization's future. Good spiritual managers will also mobilize others in the search for new opportunities and improvements.

    Your role as a *change agent* includes:

    _____

    _____

    _____

    _____

2. As **disturbance handlers,** spiritual managers deal with sudden crises that cannot be ignored, as distinguished from problems that they voluntarily solve to exploit opportunities (change agent role). The crises are caused by unforeseen events, such as conflict among people, moral failure, persecution, the loss of key people, accidents, etc. This role typically requires temporary priority over all others.

    Unfortunately, handling disturbances is all that some managers ever do. They go from crisis to crisis, reacting to circumstances. The more accurately a manager can perceive the reality of the crisis, the better he will be able to resist spending all his time consumed by such matters.

Your role as a *disturbance handler* includes:

_____

_____

_____

_____

3. The **resource allocator** role pertains to taking responsibility for allocating resources such as money, people, material, equipment, facilities and services. Spiritual managers must decide how best to use the organization's resources to attain the desired outcomes. The manager must decide which projects receive budget allocations, which of several people problems to deal with next, and even how to spend his own time.

Conceptual skills are very important here. There are rarely enough resources to go around, so the effective manager must be able to see the big picture – not just his own narrow interests – and prioritize accordingly.

Your role as a *resource allocator* includes:

_____

_____

_____

_____

4. As **negotiators**, spiritual managers formally negotiate with others, in various contexts (both positive and negative), to attain outcomes for their unit of responsibility. This negotiation may be with the senior leadership of the organization, or with other managers from other subunits, or within their own unit.

Your role as a *negotiator* includes:

_____

_____

_____

_____

Now rate yourself. For these eleven roles, which two or three are you strongest in?

_____

_____

_____

_____

Which two or three are you weakest in?

_____

_____

_____

_____

Please ask those who know you and those who work with you which managerial roles you are strongest and weakest in. What do they say?

_____

_____

_____

_____

How can you improve? Please be specific.

_____

_____

_____

## Summary of Manager Roles

| Category | Role | Activity |
|---|---|---|
| **People Roles** | Leader | Direct, encourage, train, counsel and communicate with those under his responsibility. |
| | Shepherd | Provide pastoral care to those under his responsibility. |
| | Liaison | Establish and maintain information links both inside and outside the organization. |
| | Figurehead | Perform official and legal duties on behalf of everyone else. |
| **Information Roles** | Monitor | Seek information to discover problems and opportunities. |
| | Disseminator | Forward information internally. |
| | Spokesperson | Transmit information externally. |
| **Decision Making Roles** | Change Agent | Initiate improvements projects, identify new ideas, delegate idea responsibilities to others. |
| | Disturbance Handler | Deal with crises, resolve conflicts, take corrective action during disputes. |
| | Resource Allocator | Schedule, budget, set priorities, decide who gets resources. |
| | Negotiator | Represent interests of unit during negotiations with others. |

# chapter 5

# The Skills of Spiritual Managers

The tasks of a spiritual manager are complex and multidimensional and require a range of skills. These necessary skills can be summed up in three categories: conceptual, people and technical.

Although the degree of each skill necessary at different levels of an organization may vary,[8] all managers must possess skills in each of these important areas to function effectively.

## Conceptual Skills

Conceptual skills involve the cognitive ability to see the organization as a whole and the relationships among its parts. Conceptual skills involve the manager's thinking, information processing and planning abilities. They involve knowing where one's department fits into the whole organization and how the organization fits into the broader external environment. These skills involve the ability to "think strategically" – to take the broad, long-term view.

Conceptual skills are needed by all managers but are especially important for managers at the top. They must be able to perceive significant elements in a situation and broad, conceptual patterns.

---

[8] For example, higher level managers usually need conceptual skills more than they need technical skills, while lower level managers need technical skills more than conceptual ones.

As managers move up the organizational hierarchy, they must develop conceptual skills or their effectiveness will be severely limited. A top manager who is mired in technical matters rather than thinking strategically will not do well. Many of the responsibilities of top managers, such as decision making, resource allocation, and innovation, require a broad view.

How strong are your conceptual skills?[9] Please consider the following questions and note ideas regarding strengths and weaknesses, as well as your plans for improvement.

When you have a number of tasks to do, can you set priorities and organize the work around the deadlines?

_____

_____

_____

When you are deciding on a particular course of action (such as which languages to study, job to take, special projects to be involved in), do you typically consider the long-term (three years or more) implications of what you choose to do?

_____

_____

_____

---

[9] For most of these questions, a strong "yes" answer will indicate strength in that area. Some questions, however, are asked in reverse. For these questions, which are marked, a strong "no" will indicate strength in that particular skill.

When you have a project or assignment to accomplish, do you get into the details rather than the "big picture" issues?[10]

_____

_____

_____

When you are learning something new, do you relate what you are learning to other concepts you have learned elsewhere?

_____

_____

_____

Do you have long-term visions for your ministry, family and other activities? Do you think about these visions carefully and frequently?

_____

_____

_____

Does talking about ideas and concepts get you passionate and excited?

_____

_____

_____

---

[10] This question is asked in reverse. Thus, a strong "no" answer will indicate strength in conceptual skills.

# People Skills

People skills are the manager's ability to work with and through other people and to work effectively as a group member. These skills are demonstrated in the way a person relates to others, including the ability to encourage, facilitate, coordinate, lead, communicate and resolve conflicts. A manager with good people skills allows others to express themselves without fear of rejection or ridicule and encourages participation. Such a person likes other people and is liked by them. People skills are particularly necessary in a multicultural situation.

Effective managers are cheerleaders, facilitators, coaches and nurturers. They build through people. Strong people skills enable managers to unleash others' energy and potential, and help them grow as future managers and leaders.

How strong are your people skills? Please consider the following questions and note ideas regarding strengths and weaknesses, as well as your plans for improvement.

Would most people describe you as being a good listener?

_____

_____

_____

When you have a serious disagreement with someone, do you hang in there and talk it out until it is completely resolved?

_____

_____

_____

Do you try to include others in activities or when there are discussions?

_____

_____

_____

When someone makes a mistake, do you immediately want to correct the person and let him know the proper answer or approach?[11]

_____

_____

_____

When you are working on a group project and someone isn't doing his or her fair share of the work, are you more likely to complain to your friends rather than confronting the individual?[12]

_____

_____

_____

---

[11] This question is asked in reverse. Thus, a strong "no" answer will indicate strength in people skills.
[12] This question is asked in reverse. Thus, a strong "no" answer will indicate strength in people skills.

Do projects interest you more than people?[13]

## Technical Skills

A technical skill is the understanding of and proficiency in the performance of specific tasks. Such skills include mastery of the methods, techniques and equipment involved in specific functions such as maintenance, technology or finance. These skills also include specialized knowledge, analytical ability and the competent use of tools and techniques to solve problems in that specific area.

Technical skills are particularly important at lower organizational levels. Many managers rise to their first management position by having excellent technical skills. However, technical skills become less important than people and conceptual skills as one's organizational responsibility increases.

How strong are your technical skills? Please consider the following questions and note ideas regarding strengths and weaknesses, as well as your plans for improvement.

Do you prefer to learn technical or practical things rather than those things involving concepts and ideas?

---

[13] This question is asked in reverse. Thus, a strong "no" answer will indicate strength in people skills.

Would you rather sit in front of your computer than spend a lot of time with people?

_____

_____

_____

Do you try to be efficient with your time when talking with someone, rather than worry about the other person's needs, so that you can get on with your real work?

_____

_____

_____

When solving problems, would you rather analyze some information than meet with a group of people?

_____

_____

_____

## Group Exercise

Think of two managers you have known – the best and the worst. You may have personally worked with them or you may have simply observed them.

Write down a couple of sentences to describe each of them:

The best manager I have known was…

_____

_____

_____

The worst manager I have known was…

_____

_____

_____

Now, in your small group, share your experiences (please do not name the worst manager). Each group should choose a couple of examples to share with the whole group. When you are all finished sharing, complete this table:

|  | Management roles that were fulfilled or failed in | Skills that were evident or missing | Lessons we should learn | Advice new managers should be given |
|---|---|---|---|---|
| The best managers |  |  |  |  |
| The worst managers |  |  |  |  |

## chapter 6

# The Biblical Basis of the Distinction Between Leaders and Managers

Several New Testament passages give a broad division of "ministry" into these two general dimensions of leadership and management:

> *In those days when the number of disciples was increasing, the Grecian Jews among them complained against the Hebraic Jews because their widows were being overlooked in the daily distribution of food. So the Twelve gathered all the disciples together and said, "It would not be right for us to neglect the ministry of the word of God in order to wait on tables. Brothers, choose seven men from among you who are known to be full of the Spirit and wisdom. We will turn this responsibility over to them and will give our attention to prayer and the ministry of the word." (Acts 6:1-4)*

This was not a "religious/secular" distinction, but rather a distinction along the lines of leader/manager. The apostles knew they needed to focus on the big picture issues of meaning and direction for the newly created church, so they appointed these "spiritual managers" here to take care of the daily administrative tasks.

From several New Testament Scriptures (Acts 20:17,[14] 28[15]; Titus 1:5,[16] 7[17]; 1 Peter 5:1-2[18]) we see that "elder" and "overseer" are equivalent terms for the same leadership office, and that an overseer is to "shepherd" the flock of God. This "shepherding" includes teaching (1 Tim. 3:2; 5:17; Tit. 1:9), "managing" and "caring for" the local church (1 Tim. 3:4-5; 5:17).

The office of deacon (1 Tim. 3:8; Phil. 1:1) probably emerged as the church grew in size and the leaders needed to delegate certain responsibilities. Teaching and ruling are not mentioned in connection with the deacons. Such "servants" were likely charged with caring for the church's daily practical needs (the chosen men of Acts 6:1-6 may have been prototypical of these deacons), although they also were active in spiritual ministry (cf. Acts 6:9-10; 8:5ff). Primary responsibility for the spiritual life of the church, however, probably lay with the elders.

In Philippians 1, there is this idea of two broad kinds of leadership roles in the church:

> *Paul and Timothy, servants of Christ Jesus, To all the saints in Christ Jesus at Philippi, together with the overseers and deacons: (Phil. 1:1)*

While the overseers probably gave general oversight to the church community, the deacons probably had responsibilities to serve in specific practical ways.

Thus, there were two kinds of oversight in the local churches: the general spiritual leadership of the elders and the more practical management of the deacons.

---

[14] From Miletus, Paul sent to Ephesus for the elders of the church. (Acts 20:17)
[15] Keep watch over yourselves and all the flock of which the Holy Spirit has made you overseers. Be shepherds of the church of God, which he bought with his own blood. (Acts 20:28)
[16] The reason I left you in Crete was that you might straighten out what was left unfinished and appoint elders in every town, as I directed you. (Tit. 1:5)
[17] Since an overseer is entrusted with God's work... (Tit. 1:7)
[18] To the elders among you, I appeal as a fellow elder, a witness of Christ's sufferings and one who also will share in the glory to be revealed: Be shepherds of God's flock that is under your care, serving as overseers... (1 Pet. 5:1-2)

The same idea seems to be mentioned briefly by Peter:

> *If anyone speaks, he should do it as one speaking the very words of God. If anyone serves, he should do it with the strength God provides, so that in all things God may be praised through Jesus Christ... (1 Pet. 4:11)*

As in Acts 6, Peter gives a broad, general division of ministry into that of the Word (to give overall direction regarding the "big picture") and that of "serving tables."

There are many other biblical examples. For example:

- Moses came from Mt. Sinai with the vision from God for the tabernacle. Then the managers took over responsibility for its actual building.
- In Exodus 18, Jethro helped Moses institute an effective management system for the delegation of daily tasks.
- When the Levitical priesthood was established, there was a clear division of labor as well as a hierarchy of responsibility (Num. 18:1-4, especially v. 3a).
- Solomon led in the building of the temple, but the actual work was overseen on a daily basis by others.

Jesus Himself delegated considerable responsibilities to His disciples:

> *I will give you the keys of the kingdom of heaven; whatever you bind on earth will be bound in heaven, and whatever you loose on earth will be loosed in heaven. (Matt. 16:19)*

> *If you forgive anyone his sins, they are forgiven; if you do not forgive them, they are not forgiven. (John 20:23)*

> *And these signs will accompany those who believe: In my name they will drive out demons... they will place their hands on sick people, and they will get well. (Mark 16:17-18)*

*Then Jesus came to them and said, "All authority in heaven and on earth has been given to me. Therefore [you] go and make disciples of all nations..." (Matt. 28:18-19)*

## chapter 7

# Practical Implications of the Distinction Between Leaders and Managers

1. Both leadership and management are legitimate and necessary.

   Management is about coping with *complexity*. Without good management, complex organizations – as today's churches and Christian organizations have become – tend to degenerate into chaos in ways that threaten their very existence. Good management brings order and consistency to the overall flow of life and activity in the organization. Consequently, we must have good management!

   Leadership, on the other hand, is about coping with *change* – and a church or Christian organization that is truly alive in the purposes of God will be constantly growing and maturing, and therefore changing.

   In a military analogy, a peacetime army can usually survive with good management and administration throughout the organization, coupled with a few good leaders right at the very top. An army that is at war, however, needs competent leadership at every level. No one has yet determined how to manage people effectively into battle; they must be led! The church is in a continual war. Consequently, we must have good leadership!

Leaders establish the right and powerful vision of the future. Managers keep things going smoothly while we are getting there. Leaders need managers or else they will never get where they want to go, and managers need leaders or else they will often not know where to go. Therefore, one is not superior to the other.

2. Both leaders and managers are necessary for success in fulfilling the purposes of God. Therefore, they must respect one another and learn to work together. They should complement one another and not compete.

Today's managers have been done a great disservice by contemporary leadership literature that implies or states:

- Leaders are cool, but managers are boring.
- Leadership is glamorous, mysterious and exotic, while management is mundane and tedious.
- Leadership is the province of a chosen few who possess "charisma" or other mystical personality traits, while managers are "a dime-a-dozen."
- Leaders are significant, but managers are commonplace.
- Leadership changes the world, but management is just like rearranging the deck-chairs on the Titanic.
- Leadership is fundamentally "better" than management.

In reality, we must have both leaders and managers or else we will fail.

> *The eye cannot say to the hand, "I don't need you!" And the head cannot say to the feet, "I don't need you!" On the contrary, those parts of the body that seem to be weaker are indispensable, (1 Cor. 12:21-22)*

Moreover, it is not appropriate for one to exalt himself over the other since it was God who made each of us the way we are:

> *For who makes you different from anyone else? What do you have that you did not receive? And if you did receive it, why do you boast as though you did not? (1 Cor. 4:7)*

Managers sometimes accuse leaders of being "out of touch" or "out of control" or "living in a dream world," and leaders sometimes accuse managers of "going nowhere" and "wasting everyone's time and energy with trifling details," but they need each other.

Leaders and managers must learn to work together as a team, with each contributing their unique perspective and strengths.

While most churches are overmanaged and underled, it should be remembered that strong leadership with weak management is no better, and is sometimes worse, than the reverse. Some people who are very strong in leadership abilities such as change, innovation and vision casting, lack the ability or desire to focus on tasks related to effective management. Preferring "big picture" activities to routine work, they may invest little of their time and attention in designing effective systems of administration, establishing standards, policies and procedures, or structuring roles and responsibilities. In addition, their informal, impulsive style may frequently disrupt the ongoing, legitimate activities of the organization.

The real challenge is to combine strong leadership and strong management and allow each to balance the other. Effective top leadership teams understand and value both kinds of people and work hard to make each of them an integral part of the team. Otherwise, chaos will result in the loosely-structured organization commonly associated with the strong leader.

3. Everyone needs both orientations to some degree.

While it is useful to differentiate between the roles of management and leadership, it is not helpful to view managers and leaders as entirely distinct types of people. Very few people are entirely one or the other.

One's individual style will actually be the result of a very complex interaction between one's personality, culture, gender, age, physical condition, leader/manager orientation, genes, life experiences, relationships, role models, mentors, family heritage, current family, spiritual gifts, motivational gifts, ministry gifts, formal education, and training experiences.

Regarding leader/manager orientation, everyone will be found somewhere on the following continuum:

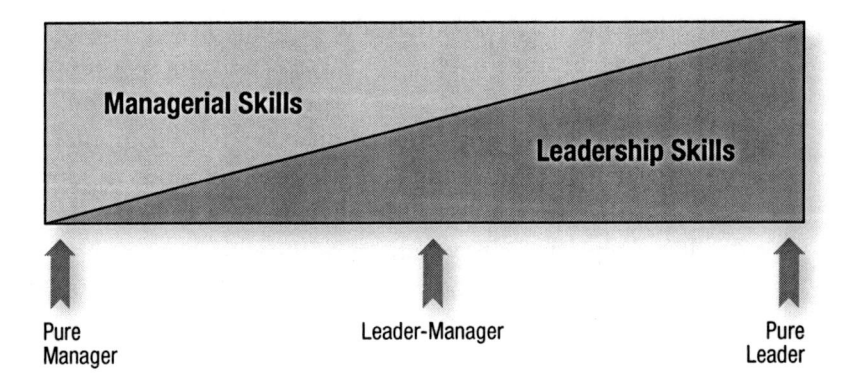

**Managerial Skills**  ⟶  **Leadership Skills**

↑ Pure Manager  ↑ Leader-Manager  ↑ Pure Leader

You should understand your strengths and weaknesses. Then you should function primarily according to your strengths while working to strengthen your weaknesses.

There is much leadership in management (the visionary and inspirational part) and much management in leadership (the detail and implementation part). Thus, the more a leader works on his managerial skills the more effective he will become, and vice-versa.

Additionally you should populate your team according to your weaknesses. Some leaders make the terrible mistake of staffing their team with people who are just like themselves. The wise leader will surround himself with people whose strengths make up for his own weaknesses.

Jesus, of course, was perfect in both capacities. He was the consummate visionary Leader (e.g., Matt. 4:19; 28:18-20) as well as the perfect Manager who attended to the details (e.g., Matt. 8:14-15; 15:32-37; 17:27).

4. There is the need for the combination leader-manager to go between leaders and managers.

Some recent literature implies that people cannot manage *and* lead, and that we must be one or the other. The effective leadership team will ignore this faulty thinking and work on identifying and developing leader-managers.

Essentially, there are three broad time frames:

- Long range (vision).
- Medium range (planning).
- The day-to-day activities of the church or organization (oversight).

An organization that only has visionary leaders (long range) and effective managers (day-to-day activities) will experience a lot of conflict.

There needs to be the leader-manager to bridge the gap: one who is comfortable in both worlds, and who can effectively relate and connect the long-range vision to the daily realities of the organization.

Thus, leaders invest time on the vision. Leader-managers put the flesh on the bones and make practical and realistic plans, while managers then efficiently implement and administrate those plans on a daily basis.[19]

The relationships of all three roles to both planning and time are depicted in the following graphic:

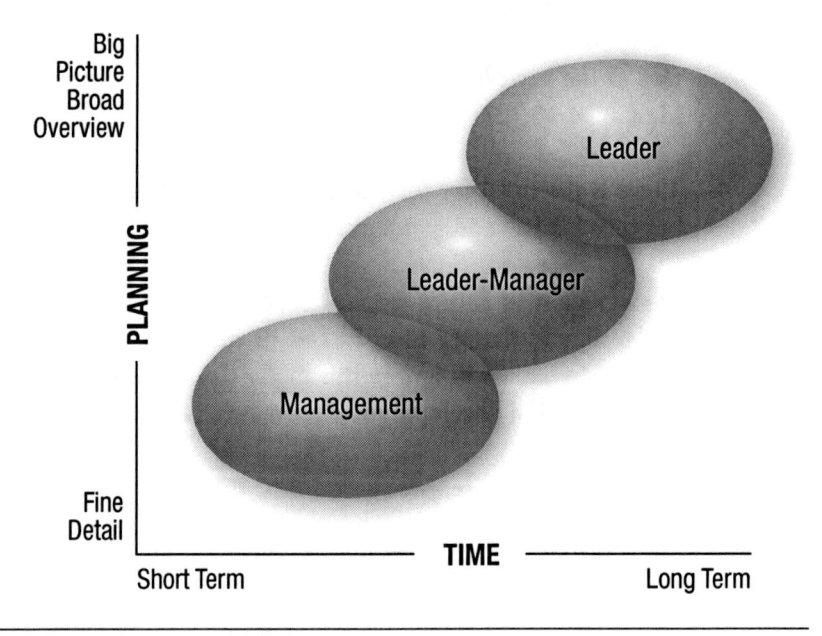

```
Big
Picture
Broad
Overview                              Leader

   PLANNING              Leader-Manager

              Management


Fine
Detail
              Short Term    TIME    Long Term
```

---

[19] Other models may use different terminology for these three roles. For example, they may speak of the leader (my leader), the manager (my leader-manager) and the administrator (my manager). The underlying principles regarding the three roles remain essentially the same. Additionally, in certain languages these terms may differ also. For example, in Spanish it would be better to speak of leader, leader-administrator, and administrator.

It is obviously important that all three ovals receive attention: we need a vision, a strategy and tactical details to be provided by leaders, leader-managers and managers respectively.

- Leaders provide vision.
- Leader-managers provide strategy.
- Managers provide tactical details.

Moreover, as the following graphic demonstrates, an effective leader-manager is able to produce powerful synergies between the two roles.

# The Synergies of an Effective Leader-Manager

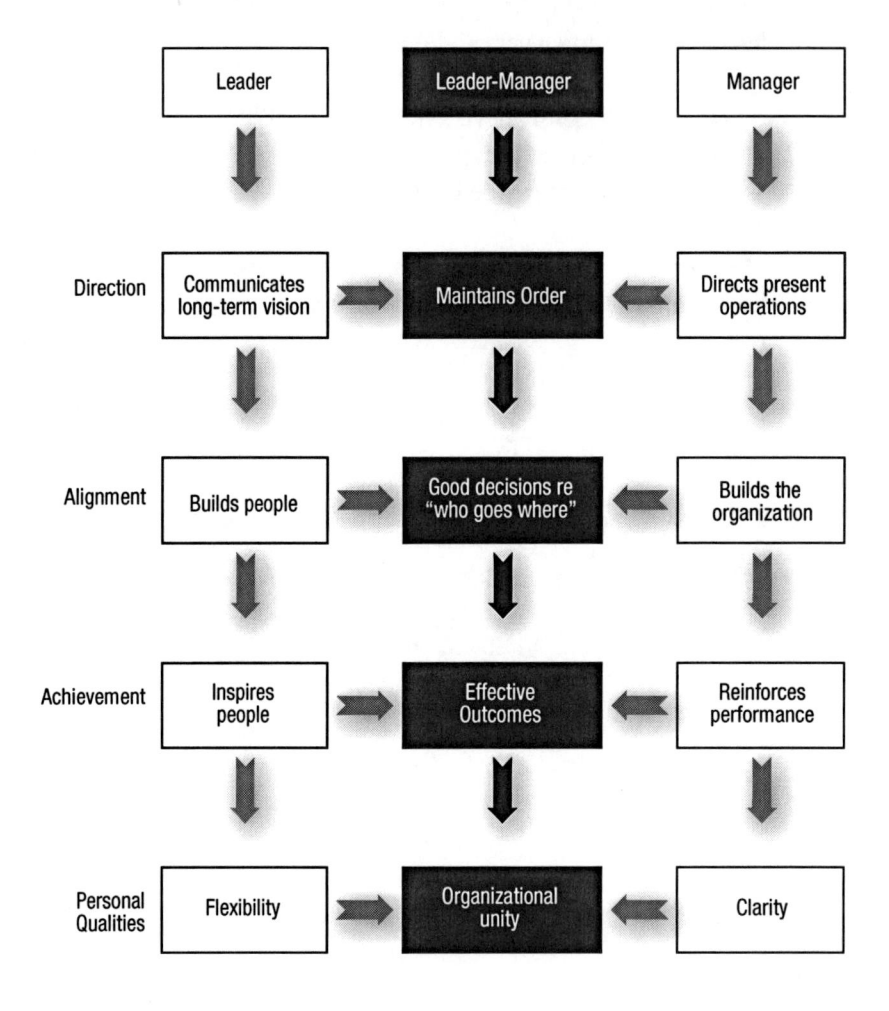

| | Leader | Leader-Manager | Manager |
|---|---|---|---|
| Direction | Communicates long-term vision | Maintains Order | Directs present operations |
| Alignment | Builds people | Good decisions re "who goes where" | Builds the organization |
| Achievement | Inspires people | Effective Outcomes | Reinforces performance |
| Personal Qualities | Flexibility | Organizational unity | Clarity |

In balancing the big picture and long-term vision with the demands of the present operations, the leader-manager is able to maintain order.

Then the leader-manager works with both the development of people and the needs of the organization so that effective decisions regarding alignment can be made.

By both inspiring and directing people, the leader-manager contributes to the organization's success.

Finally, through his personal make-up that balances flexibility and an ability to work with ambiguity on the one hand and managerial clarity on the other, the leader-manager is able to bring unity to the organization, building bridges between the visionaries and the administrators, between the big picture and the fine details.

5. In general, the particular situation of an organization serves as a context for leading and managing, determining which orientation is appropriate and which set of skills is needed at any time. This situation can be difficult to assess because it can be a moving target!

   One model of organizational development proposes five stages in the normal cycle of organizational life: form, storm, norm, perform and reform. These stages are generally true for any organization or organizational subunit (such as a new church plant, or a new ministry being developed within an existing church).

   - The *form* stage is concerned with the mission, vision, goals and overall structure of the organization.

   - The *storm* stage involves establishing individual roles and responsibilities. During this time the focus is on interpersonal relationships and communication, and the concentration is on team building, conflict resolution, problem solving and decision making.

- The *norm* stage is concerned with establishing organization and group processes, procedures, methods and standards.

- During the *perform* stage, the organization "gets down to business" and becomes good at what it is aiming to accomplish.

- The fifth stage of *reform* is necessary to continuously renew the organization and keep it on the cutting edge of the will of God. At this point, when the vision is fulfilled or changes, the process starts over, going from perform back to form.

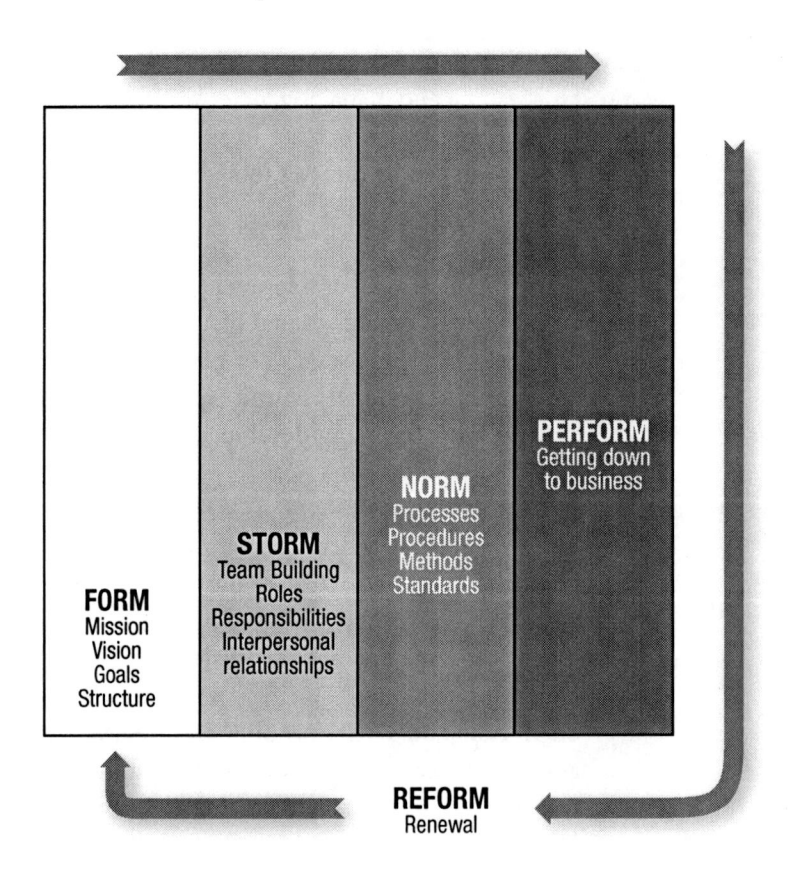

**FORM**
Mission
Vision
Goals
Structure

**STORM**
Team Building
Roles
Responsibilities
Interpersonal relationships

**NORM**
Processes
Procedures
Methods
Standards

**PERFORM**
Getting down to business

**REFORM**
Renewal

To be effective, each stage of organizational development requires a different mix on the leader-manager continuum.

At the *form* stage, when a project is beginning, a new strategy is created, or a new organization has begun, leadership is key. Vision must be formed and communicated, leadership teams must be formed, and people must be encouraged and inspired.

At the *storm* stage, a combination of leadership and management is critical. There is a strong need to focus others on the mission, build networks, and apply interpersonal skills, especially around resolving conflict; but now the manager needs to emerge to put structure into place, begin to identify needed skills and experience and provide constant feedback.

At the *norm* stage, management abilities move to the forefront. The organization needs the administration of planning, staffing and setting goals to fulfill the vision established at the first.

At the *perform* stage, the manager must fully emerge to maintain and improve daily operations, with the appropriate systems and processes all in place.

At the fifth stage of *reform*, the leader once again begins to emerge to institute necessary organizational change, and the cycle starts again.

| Stage | Orientation |
|---|---|
| Form | Leading |
| Storm | Leading and managing |
| Norm | Managing and leading |
| Perform | Managing |
| Reform | Leading |

The next graphic illustrates the leader-manager mix throughout the organizational cycle.

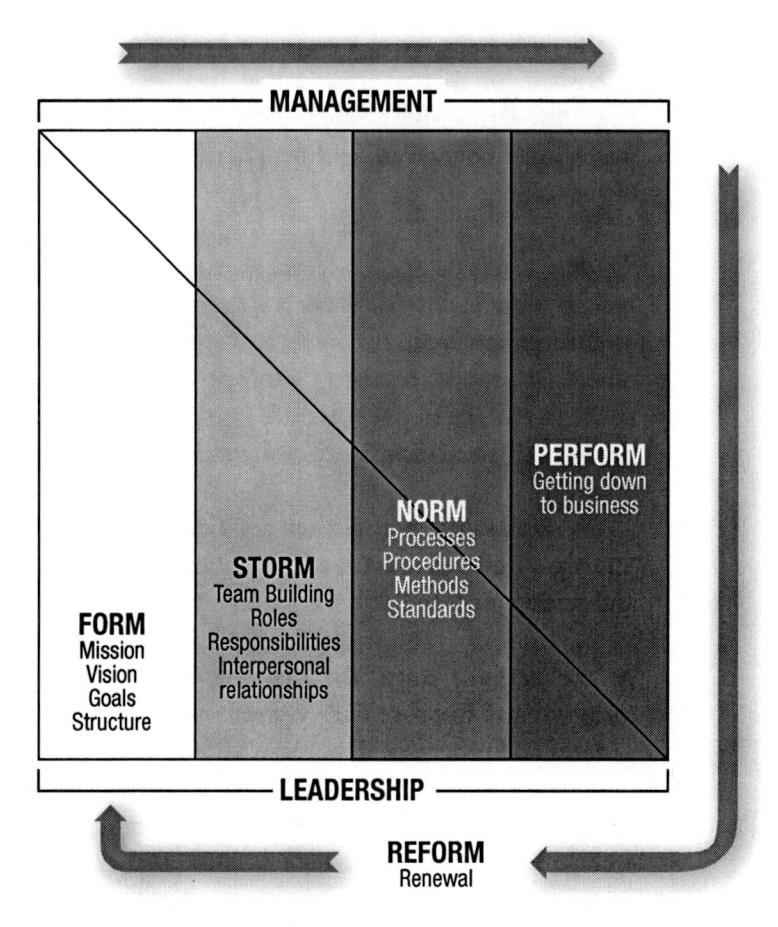

**MANAGEMENT**

**FORM**
Mission
Vision
Goals
Structure

**STORM**
Team Building
Roles
Responsibilities
Interpersonal
relationships

**NORM**
Processes
Procedures
Methods
Standards

**PERFORM**
Getting down
to business

**LEADERSHIP**

**REFORM**
Renewal

6. Considering our graphic relating to time and planning, one must not spend time in Zone A (see below). The urgency of the short-term requires detailed plans that lead to immediate action and accomplishment.

Similarly, Zone B is also unproductive and inefficient for leaders. There is no point in drawing up detailed plans applying to a few years away. Unless God has given you an exact and detailed description of the future, your visionary skills are probably not good enough to warrant this. There will be unforeseen events that you did not predict, and nearer the time, your detailed plans will have to be redone.

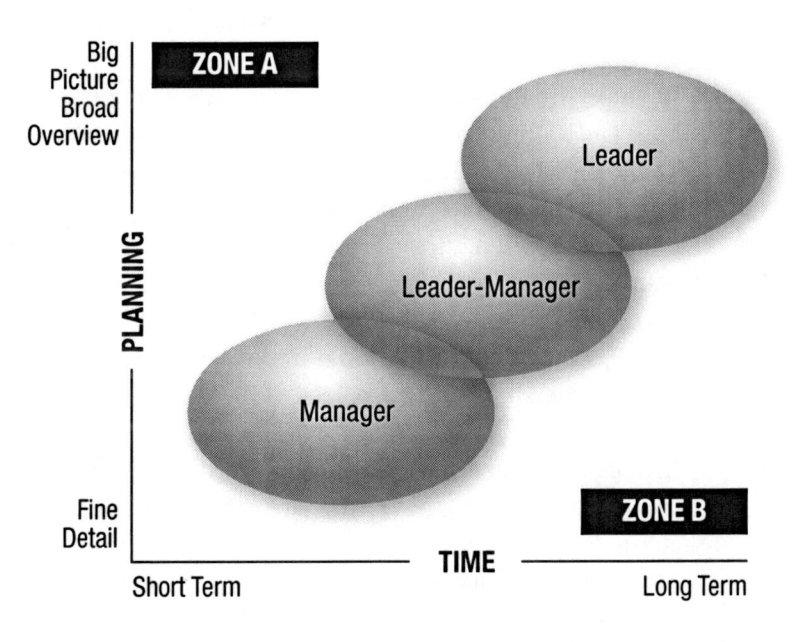

*Diagram: Planning zones showing Manager (short term, fine detail), Leader-Manager (middle), and Leader (long term, big picture broad overview). Zone A is upper-left; Zone B is lower-right.*

7. Determine what God's calling is for your life. Then, find that place and do it well.

God has given each of us the right gifts so we can fulfill His particular will for our lives.

> *All these are the work of one and the same Spirit, and he gives them to each one, just as he determines. The body is a unit, though it is made up of many parts; and though all its parts are many, they form one body. So it is with Christ. (1 Cor. 12:11-12)*

God made you what you are: your personality, your gifts and talents, your experiences all contribute to the unique person that you are now. Be who you are, and do it well! That's what counts. Leadership may appear on the surface to be more glamorous, but if it is not what God has called you to do, you are wasting precious time pursuing something that is not God's will. "The pay is the same in the end!"

8. In some situations, men and women with strong leadership gifts and callings have been forced into managerial modes. Their organizational environments or even national cultures (e.g., in Japan) have only ever allowed or encouraged the managerial orientation. Frustration and failure inevitably result.

9. There is much confusion today about what constitutes true "team leadership."

In a team, we can have those who are strong in leadership characteristics and those who are strong in management characteristics and those in-between. As each person finds his appropriate place in the flow of things, the team will do well.

If the team, however, makes all the visionary, "big-picture" decisions by unanimous agreement (if that is one's conception of "team leadership"), then many times those decisions will be the wrong ones since they will be made by managers, whose abilities and priorities are fundamentally different from leaders.

We need balance in the team. The leaders need to make the leadership decisions (tempered with input from the managers). The managers need to make the management decisions (tempered with input from the leaders). Together it works very well.[20]

---

[20] Of course, each needs to receive input from the other and there must be genuine accountability in place.

Often, managers in a team will want the leader or leaders to be "accountable." Certainly the leader must be accountable. But this is not accomplished by putting managers in charge of the leader's decisions!

If that happens, the organization will never go anywhere. The leaders will want to move ahead but the managers who are typically more cautious and less comfortable with the inescapable ambiguity of the future will be given veto power by virtue of the simple fact that a unanimous agreement is required to make a decision.

Thus, what is popularly called "team leadership" in many circles is, in reality, "team management."

Managers should allow leaders to make the leadership decisions, and leaders should allow managers to make management decisions. And those with a strong leadership-management mix in their abilities should clearly understand the nature of the particular decision that is before them and make that decision accordingly. In a prayerful spirit of mutual understanding and submission, such a strategy works well.

10. The distinction between leaders and managers should not be used as an excuse for sloppiness or lack of diligence and responsibility on the part of the leader. Unfortunately, it sometimes is. Some leaders do not even try to improve their management skills, leaving all the details and responsibilities for the daily life of the organization up to others to worry about.

Moreover, many people seek leadership roles since those roles appear easier than management roles. Consequently, we end up with many leaders who do not have adequate leadership skills or are very sloppy and careless in their lives and ministries. Not having the true inner disciplines of leadership in place in their lives, it is as if they were driving a car without a clear destination. They just, as it were, get in the car and start driving down the road. Then they get an impulse that they should turn here, and so they veer off in that direction, then later decide that it would be good to turn there, and so they swerve off in that direction. They constantly "fly by the seat of their pants," and half the time they go in circles. They may generate a lot of hype and excitement in the process, but they never really accomplish anything or lead anyone anywhere. Such leaders are usually able to spiritualize their personal disorganization. They often justify that kind of personal lifestyle and leadership as "being led by the Spirit." In reality, they are as "reeds shaken in the wind," "blown about by every wind of doctrine."

The truth is that good leadership is just as disciplined a process as management is – perhaps more so – and it usually carries greater responsibility.

11. Managers look at successful leadership and instead see organizational form. This is the way managers often view successful leadership.

A great leader comes along, understands his situation, receives a great vision from God and does "the stuff," growing a successful church or ministry.

Other leaders will look at him, to see what aspects of leadership they can learn better from him. Managers, however, look at him, study his "system" and copy it, thinking that the power lies in the system. Then they imitate the procedure, which, of course, rarely works as well as for them as it did for him.[21]

The reason the leader was successful was not because of the particular system he used. It was because he was a leader who had the right vision from God for his time and place.

---

[21] Some prominent recent examples in the western church would include seeker-friendly services, cell groups, etc.

What we need is not successful systems, but *leaders* in the right places at the right times. Sometimes it is hard for managers to truly understand or appreciate this. They are continually looking for the "right system." The management mentality is: If we can just get the right system in place, then it will work. That is wrong! You must have the right *leader* in place. Then he will initiate whatever system or form may be appropriate for those people at that time in that place. Systems are subordinate to leadership. People make organizations successful – not systems.[22]

The workman (the leader) does need the right tools (systems, structure, organizational design, etc.), but the skill is in the hands of the workman, not the tools. Therefore, our primary focus should be on the development of leaders, and not merely the development of the right tools.

In a manner of speaking, a good leader could make *any* structure or system work. The form is not the issue; leadership is the issue.

12. Many times visionary leaders give their managers projects to accomplish that the managers know are genuinely unrealistic. For example, the manager may recognize that the organization's resources are already stretched beyond their capacity and the new project simply cannot successfully be undertaken. How should the manager respond in such a situation? Often, exasperated managers will respond negatively to their leaders by simply telling them, "We can't do this. You're asking too much. We simply can't do it all."

---

[22] I visited a very large church several years ago. At that time there were around 5000 people in the main church and they had started some other churches around the city. In a meeting with one of the church's leaders, I correctly guessed that these daughter churches which had all been started by protégés of the main leader would be much smaller than the main church, even though they used the same strategies and systems as the main church. Organizations don't succeed because of systems but because of leaders!

A better response is to say, "This new vision is wonderful. Let's work together to accomplish it. However, due to our existing obligations, we simply don't have the resources necessary (people, time, money, etc.) at this time to do it all. But we want to do it all, so please work with me so that we can either rearrange our existing commitments or somehow gain new resources, so that we *can* do it all." Such a response will usually be met with the favor of the leader, rather than his frustration at being simply told, "We can't do it."

This positive approach will accomplish two additional things. First, it will help the leader better connect with the daily organizational realities that the manager lives with. Second, it will help the manager better connect with the future possibilities that the visionary leader lives with.

13. Not everyone is a leader or manager. We still need "sailors" as well as "captains"!

   *But in fact God has arranged the parts in the body, every one of them, just as he wanted them to be. If theywere all one part, where would the body be? As it is,there are many parts, but ne body. (1 Cr. 12:8-0*

# Books in the *SpiritBuilt Leadership* Series
## by Malcolm Webber, Ph.D.

1. *Leadership.* Deals with the nature of leadership, servant leadership, and other basic leadership issues.

2. *Healthy Leaders.* Presents a simple but effective model of what constitutes a healthy Christian leader.

3. *Leading.* A study of the practices of exemplary leaders.

4. *Building Leaders.* Leaders build leaders! However, leader development is highly complex and very little understood. This book examines core principles of leader development.

5. *Leaders & Managers.* Deals with the distinctions between leaders and managers. Contains extensive worksheets.

6. *Abusive Leadership.* A must read for all Christian leaders. Reveals the true natures and sources of abusive leadership and servant leadership.

7. *Understanding Change.* Leading change is one of the most difficult leadership responsibilities. It is also one of the most important. This book is an excellent primer that will help you understand resistance to change, the change process and how to help people through change.

8. *Building Teams.* What teams are and how they best work.

9. *Understanding Organizations.* A primer on organizational structure.

10. *Women in Leadership.* A biblical study concerning this very controversial issue.

11. ***Healthy Followers.*** The popular conception that "everything depends on leaders" is not entirely correct. Without thoughtful and active followers, the greatest of leaders will fail. This book studies the characteristics of healthy followers and is also a great resource for team building.

12. ***Listening.*** Listening is one of the most important of all leadership skills. This book studies how we can be better listeners and better leaders.

13. ***Transformational Thinking.*** This book introduces a new model of transformational thinking – of loving God with our minds – that identifies the critical thinking capacities of a healthy Christian leader. In addition, practical ways of nurturing those thinking capacities are described.

**Strategic Press**
www.StrategicPress.org

Strategic Press is a division of Strategic Global Assistance, Inc.
www.sgai.org

2601 Benham Avenue
Elkhart, IN 46517
U.S.A.

+1-574-295-4357
Toll-free: 888-258-7447